ISLAMIC LAW

Understanding Juristic Differences

ISLAMIC LAW

Understanding Juristic Differences

By

Ahmad Zaki Hammad, Ph.D.

American Trust Publications

Indianapolis

To Salma, Osama, & their mother and grandparents

American Trust Publications & the Author
10900 W. Washington St. • Indianapolis, IN 46321

ISBN Number 0-89259-074-2

CONTENTS

PREFACE

It is indeed one of the crowning achievements of Muslim civilization that for centuries and through the most unpredictable times of expansion and racial and cultural diversification Muslims were able to resist that most dreaded of impulses, to which religious communities are otherwise so notoriously predisposed: To seek unity and order within the Community by artificially fordizing its beliefs and practices. Indeed, so striking was this feature of Muslim civilization that it could not fail to capture the attention of even non-Muslim observers in the West, such as Ignaz Goldziher:

> In considering the origins and historical development of early Islam, one general fact, whose proper appreciation is crucial for an understanding of the development of Islam, must not escape our attention. The fact that I have in mind is the complete absence of any dogmatic impulse. Despite the tendency toward uniformity which

occasionally manifested itself, the acceptance of "legitimate particularity" (*berechtiger Eigentumlichkeiten*) always triumphed.[1]

One need not be detained here by the phrase "legitimate particularity"; nor need its non-Muslim origins be cause for alarm. What is important is the *historical fact* that our Muslim ancestors accepted and applied this as a principle, especially in the area of Law (*fiqh*); that is, though a doctrine or practice might be particular to a specific group or individual, this alone was not sufficient to deny it recognition as a bona fide constituent of the religion of God, nor to deny its adherents the privilege of freely advocating and practicing it, nor to impugn or call into question their level of commitment as believing, practicing Muslims.

In the present work, Dr. Ahmad Zaki Hammad makes a stunning contribution to the restoration of "legitimate particularity" among Muslims, by laying bare the issue of *juristic differences*, known in Arabic as *khilâf*. By explaining the legitimate causes of juristic difference and distinguishing those forms that are legitimate from those that are not, Dr. Hammad guides his reader to a fascinating rediscovery of the spirit of tolerance and mutual recognition in Islam. His many examples, featuring some of the most illustrious and authoritative names in Muslim history, show that far from being a voguish innovation spawned by the chaos of modern times, "legitimate particularity" is a call from the very depths of the Islamic tradition, a veritable hallmark of the faith itself.

Dr. Hammad has not limited his audience to either immigrant or indigenous Muslims; indeed, both groups stand to benefit greatly from a sincere and open-minded reading of this work. He has taken great care to be as circumspect as necessary, without, meanwhile, overburdening his reader with cumbersome jargon and details. This renders the work pleasantly unpresumptuous and inviting to both the expert and the layperson alike.

In these our times, few would deny the need for greater understanding and tolerance among Muslims. To this end, Dr. Hammad's work takes a bold and important step. May Allah bless him for his fine contribution. And may He grant us the courage and patience to listen and then act according to the best of what we hear.

In the end, of course, all praise is to Allah, who guides from among His servants whomsoever He pleases. May He guide us all to that which pleases Him and shower His blessings upon our beloved Prophet, Muḥammad b. 'Abd Allah.

Abd al-Hakim S. Jackson, Ph.D.
University of Texas, Austin

INTRODUCTION

Experiencing the study and practice of Islamic Law among Muslims and non-Muslims, East and West, has refined my appreciation for an essential need: It is incumbent upon those who believe in the inevitability of Islamic revival (despite differing approaches), as it is essential for academicians in the field, to distinguish between three facets of Islam with regard to its Law, namely, *Revelation*, *Interpretation*, and *Application*.

Revelation comprises the Islamic Texts as expressed in (1) the Quran, the Book of Allah recorded and recited in the established recitations and (2) the Sunna, the traditions of the Prophet Muḥammad, upon him be peace, narrated in authentic reports. Revelation, naturally, has been expressed in human languages. As a standing linguistic miracle, the Quran exalted Arabic literature and rhetoric to the peaks of eloquence and inspired an unfathomable burst of knowledge and inquiry.

Interpretation in this context is the human understanding resulting from continuous and insightful engagement with the Texts. It is the wellspring of the religious sciences, which include law (*fiqh*) and its principles (*uṣûl*), Quranic commentary (*tafsîr*), and the study of the Prophetic model and teachings.

Application, then, is the human act of translating the Islamic Texts into a way of life, with all that this implies in terms of practical guidance, morality, and legislation.

I have witnessed the misbegotten consequences resulting from the mental mingling of these elements, both in those who 'strive' for Islam in the fog of confusion, as well as among those engaged in the study of Islam or the affairs of Muslims.

For instance, some zealous students in the United States and Canada, unwittingly, but nevertheless rigidly, hold the opinions of leading imams and scholars—i.e., their understanding and *ijtihâd*—as equal to the Book of Allah and the Sunna of His Messenger. So when one expresses a dissenting opinion unknown to them or offers an original understanding based on a comprehensive survey of the Islamic Texts or credible Islamic experience, he or she is easily charged with altering religion.

Equally injurious are those who have little or no regard for the legacy of Islamic understanding advanced by preceding Muslim authorities when it exceeds the narrow corridors of their thinking, the truncated extent of their vision, or the circular limits of their experience. Yet they boast that their loyalty and adherence are only to the verses of the Book and statements of the Prophet! In other words, what is too subtle for them is met reflexively with quarrelsome dismissal, poorly masking a voice of frustration.

In addition, many academicians in the field of Islamic studies in the West focus, out of ignorance or bias, on the incidental aspects of Muslim life within Islamic civilization. They often cite political, social, moral, or economic practices in 'this' or 'that' time, within a particular society, as defining Islam itself. Others come to Islam or turn away from it while harboring defective perceptions of its civilization and essentials.

We live in a world where calls for fairness, freedom of expression, worship, and participation in political decision-making are particularly loud. And since people are seeking a universal vision and brotherhood that will free them from the complexities of prejudice and the heritage of hate, it is both timely and necessary to understand Islam as expressed in the changeless Quran and verified Prophetic wisdom.

Islam—in every chapter of its Book and in all the teachings of its Prophet—declares itself as the Final Revelation and the divine prescription for humanity to live in peace with itself and with all creation, and, more importantly, to live in harmony with the Creator, who sustains with the greatest of ease the heavens and the earth and all therein.

I am aware that reaching this goal requires great and

ceaseless effort to return contemporary thinking, moral sensibility, and the human spirit back to the path of its Maker. Yet I share the growing realization that we possess all that it takes to fulfill this mission.

We ask Allah to make fruitful this effort to mature our attitude toward diversity in legal (*fiqhî*) approach and judgment, and discourage rigid adherence to *madhhabiyya*, i.e., confining one's loyalties to a particular scope of *fiqh*, where undue energies are spent in senseless dispute over the details of the *Sharî'a* and with blind bias regarding ideas and personalities.

Among the correspondence I have received regarding the Arabic edition of this work, a number of scholars and readers pressed for reprinting it in both Arabic and English. One prominent educator indicated he had already instructed his staff to make an audio recording of it for circulation throughout the Gulf region.

It is my hope that this edition, as well as the forthcoming *Introduction to Islamic Law*, a companion volume to Abû Ḥâmid al-Ghazâlî's monumental *al-Musṭaṣfâ min 'Ilm al-Uṣûl (The Quintessence of the Science of the Principles)*, which I have been fortunate enough to have translated into English, will help form the foundation of Islamic legal thinking among readers of English. This is coupled with another desire: To find the time and energy to return to this sensitive topic, giving it more elaborate treatment and benefiting from related works that have appeared since the Arabic edition.

Yet this book has been kept succinct in order to compress its vast topic into an attainable whole.

As for the text, the verses of the Quran interpreted into English appear in italics rather than within quotation marks. Boldface type has been used throughout to make scanning and review easy.

The book itself is composed of two parts, the first summarizing and giving background to the issue of diversity as a human and natural phenomenon, the second detailing five specific causes and classic cases of legal variance among the famous practitioners.

The four chapters have summaries that distill the particular topic of *al-khilâf al-fiqhî* (juristic difference) under discussion down to its essence. In addition, fourteen secondary subtopics make the book maximally accessible, each one a digestible apportionment.

I appreciate the efforts of Amer Haleem and Ibrahim Abusharif for their help with the English text, as well as Ibrahim Abdul Aziz for helping with part of the first draft of the translation. Also, earnest appreciation goes to my dear friend, Brother Gaylord Toft, whose insistence to make optimal use of current computer technology has saved a tremendous amount of time for this and other projects. May Allah bless him and his family.

Ahmad Zaki Hammad, Ph.D.

PART ONE

THE FOUNDATION

I. The Meaning of *Khilaf* & *Ikhtilaf*

The Arabs possess a delicate linguistic morphology and subtle ways of using it. Among other things, they apply the noun *khilâf* to a barren tree, a willow which bears no fruit. This is the tree of sterility, and the place where it grows is called *wâdî al-makhlafa*, the valley of fruitlessness. In its more common meaning, however, one that is more relevant to juristic differences in Islamic Law, *khilâf* refers to opposition, variance in opinion, and disagreement.

Ikhtilâf, a derivative of the same root as *khilâf*, means inconsonance, inconsistency, incompatibility, discordance. Al-Râghib al-Aṣfahânî, a renowned lexicographer of Quranic terminology, writes:

> *Al-ikhtilâf* and *al-mukhâlafa* denote that each thing is on a path other than the path of its counterpart, in

> state or in statement. Another of its meanings is 'inequality'; things which are not equal being certainly different and distinguished from one another....As for *khilâf*, it means 'conflict,' connoting the meaning of *ikhtilâf* and exceeding it.[2]

Aṣfahânî's definition adds that *ikhtilâf*, that is, conflicting statements, result in tension, or argument and dispute. This is indicated in the Quran: *The confederates have differed among themselves.*[3]

The technical terminology of the jurists

The majority of Muslim jurists do not distinguish in *technical* usage between the terms *khilâf* and *ikhtilâf*. They use them interchangeably when describing conflict between persons who differ in opinion, persuasion, belief, or religion. In other words, the terms indicate discord in the points of view and positions of individuals.

Still, if the motive for disagreement is selfless and informed, that is, if it is a matter of devotion to Allah, then it is ultimately beneficial, in this world and the next. But the ends of self-serving dispute are punishment and suffering, here and in the Hereafter.

Al-Shâṭibî distinguishes the term *khilâf* in this regard, defining it as "that which is grounded in vain, erroneous opinion; that in which the disputant does not pursue the will and pleasure of Allah....This occurs with Muslims as well as non-Muslims."[4]

But the term *ikhtilâf*, in his view, is narrower and

applies to the technical dispute "that occurs among *mujtahids* [practitioners of independent legal judgment] in cases that lack decisive evidence from the Law which would otherwise resolve the difference in question."

Islamic Texts and khilâf

The Quranic verses and the Prophet's utterances are unequivocal in urging Muslims to unity, solidarity, and a bonding commitment. Allah, the Exalted, states: *Hold firmly to the rope of Allah altogether, and do not become divided.*[5] Also, He says, *Truly Allah loves those who strive in His path in ranks as though they were a cemented structure.*[6]

Similarly, Allah has forbidden division and contentiousness in His statement: *Do not dispute or you will fail and lose your power; rather be patient. Indeed, Allah is with the patient.*[7] And again, *Be not like those who divided and differed after clear signs had come to them. And it is those for whom there is a great punishment.*[8]

The Prophet has warned Muslims not to become divided; for "indeed, those before you divided and they perished."[9] The Prophet also has said, "The hand of Allah is with the Community, and whosoever secedes does so into the Fire."[10]

Prohibited categories of khilâf

Khilâf (conflict), in the sense of opposition to the Sharî'a or turning away from its path and application, is a distinguishing characteristic of *kufr* (irreligiosity or, in the worst case, disbelief); from the evils of which, we seek Allah's protection. To this the Quran states, *So let those who deviate from His Commandment beware, lest they be struck by an affliction or a severe punishment.*[11] Also, it states, *Surely those who oppose Allah and His Prophet, they are the lowly.*[12]

Summary

• Divergence is a logical, if not natural, possibility that occurs among human beings. As such, the Lawmaker has prohibited its reprehensible forms.

• It is possible to take precaution and avoid diversity of the destructive kind. Were this not the case, Allah would not have made it obligatory to refrain from it. *Allah does not burden a soul beyond its capacity.*[13]

• Diversity which is sectarian in nature and blatantly factionalizing is prohibited. Whosoever intentionally participates in it, realizing its results, is subject to punishment in this world and the next: *Be not like those who divided and differed after clear signs had come to them. And it is those for whom there is a great punishment.*[14]

In acknowledging these points, what remains is a need to respond to a number of questions related to the occurrence of *khilâf*: Is legal diversification an inevitability or only a possibility? To what extent and how often does it actually happen? Also, are all its forms blameworthy, or are there kinds that are praiseworthy? What are the causes of diversity? And what are the means of safeguarding against its blameworthy types? What should be our position in regard to it?

There are additional problems that underscore the need to alleviate misunderstandings centered on juristic *khilâf*. We will address these points, with Allah's aid, presently.

II. Variation in God's Creation

In many instances, the Quran urges rational beings to observe and contemplate the overwhelming diversity in creation. Unique and variant forms and colors in our vast universe are clear signs and displays of the power of its Creator. *Surely in the creation of the heavens and the earth and the diversity of night and day are signs for those of insight.*[15] In another verse, *And of His signs is the creation of the heaven and the earth and the diversity of your languages and colors.*[16]

The diversity within humanity alone is magnificent; and it is not exhausted by such things as color of skin and varying physical structure. In fact, variation extends to qualities such as natural and acquired gifts, talents, skills, and temperaments. Even dispositions differ to the degree that each person has unique sensitivities, affinities, anxieties, and motivations.

This type of diversity—clear evidence of our Maker's splendor—may affect a person's viewpoint. Thus, established truths in your case or mine may not be accepted as truths by others. Things which we hold as certain, decisive indicators of design in the universe may be held by others as mere coincidence or luck.

Inescapable diversity

Allah establishes in the Quran that had He so willed, *He would have made people a single nation, yet they will not cease differing, except those upon whom your Lord has mercy—it is for this reason that He has created them.*[17]

Allah did not will to create a monolithic, uniform human species, equal and compatible in all ways. Rather, He cast human nature into various molds and fixed firmly in it the capacity to bear diversity.

Diversity of opinion among Muslims

It is popularly attributed to the Prophet, peace be upon him, that he said, "The Jews have split into seventy-one groups; the Christians into seventy-two; my Community will divide into seventy-three* groups—all will be in the Fire with the exception of one."[18]

This *ḥadîth* is not acceptable as a justification for sectarianism among Muslims; nor does it deny the inherent evil of it. Rather, it warns the intelligent to avoid the kind of diversity that leads to sectarianism. In order to avoid falling into this division, however, one must first acquire a firm understanding of the difference between blameworthy and acceptable forms of differing.

---

*Some interpret the use of the number "seventy" here as an Arabic idiom expressing a large number rather than an exact count.

Blameworthy diversity

Disbelief in or rejection of the Sharî'a, as stated above, is the **first** and most reprehensible type of *khilâf*, those holding that position being clearly astray.

A **second** kind of blameworthy divergence of opinion concerns false claimers, those who attribute to Islam things which Allah has not prescribed. "Various forms of error and misguidance," the Prophet said, "would emerge from a people coming forth from the East. They recite the Quran, yet it does not penetrate their beings any deeper than their throats. They fly out of Islam as arrows fly forth from their bows, and they return to Islam no more than does a spent arrow return to its archer."[19]

A **third** type of diversity takes place among the various legal schools or *madhâhib* (s. *madhhab*): The belief of some that their positions are correct and all others invalid.

A classic example of this type of diversity is the case of the tenth-century jurist Muḥammad b. Yaḥya b. Lubâba[20] of Muslim Spain, who on occasion differed from the legal opinions of Mâlik, whose school was dominant in Spain.[21] For this, Ibn Lubâba was stripped of the office of judge, put under house arrest, and forbidden to express his religious opinions.

During this time, the governor of Cordoba, "al-Nâṣir" (Abdul-Raḥmân b. Muḥammad al-Umawî) wanted to purchase a piece of land near his residence. But the land was a *waqf*,[22] or religious endowment, for the rehabilitation of the sick. Al-Nâṣir was discomforted by this use and inquired about the permissibility of its purchase, with the understanding that he would secure equal property with which to substitute the hospital.

The leading Mâlikî judge of the time, Ibn Baqîy, ruled that such a transaction would be illegal. In his view, the most important point in the case was maintaining the sacredness of the hospital as a *waqf*. Al-Nâṣir requested that the chief judge confer with the other Mâlikî jurists and inform them of his willingness to purchase the land at even a greatly increased price. But still, the governor was unable to convince them.

When Ibn Lubâba heard of this, he sent a message to al-Nâṣir, informing him that the case was more flexible than the judges had decided. If the governor could arrange a meeting between Ibn Lubâba and the council of scholars, he would present legal argument to reverse the ruling. The governor consented, and Ibn Lubâba addressed the gathering.

"The Ḥanafîs, who honor the validity of *ra'î* [rational judgement] as part of the Sharî'a, have allowed this kind of transaction," he said. "They are, of course, equally great scholars, by whom, in fact, the majority of the Muslim community is guided. Now, the head of state has a need. And in the Prophet's tradition clearly there is leniency. So in this case, I would rule in accordance with the jurists of Iraq [the Ḥanafîs]."

"Do you abandon the teachings of Mâlik," they

protested, "upon which our forefathers based their rulings until they passed, and which we likewise have adopted after them and ruled accordingly? By Allah, we will never deviate from that way in any matter!"

Ibn Lubâba responded, "I appeal to you in the name of Allah, the Magnificent! Is it not true that if a case comes before you—in which your own interests lie—that you occasionally take positions other than those of Mâlik, if it serves a need?"

"Yes," they answered.

"Then certainly the governor is more deserving."[23]

This type of rigid adherence to a legal (*fiqhî*) school—denying due justice to alternate valid legal methods and perspectives—is blameworthy because of the reluctance to concede even the possibility that another well-founded opinion may be acceptable. It is regrettable that generations have passed under the sway of such inflexible adherence to the *madhâhib*.

Let us end this discussion with a statement from a Ḥanafî scholar, al-Karkhî (d. 340/952), which illustrates the spirit of excessive commitment to one's *madhhab* (though this is not to say al-Karkhî's thinking was not governed by higher principles):

> The guiding principle with us [Ḥanafîs] is that every Quranic verse which differs from our legal school must be interpreted as either being abrogated or preponderated. The preferable option is that it be interpreted loosely in order to adjust it to the school's interpretation. In principle, every statement in dispute of a similar ruling of ours must be considered

countered by our proof, so as to accommodate the school's final position.

Praiseworthy diversity

Allah and His Prophet have commanded the Muslim to differentiate him- or herself from pagans or advocates or holders of erroneous beliefs and behavior. In a number of *ḥadîths*, Muslims are bid to distinguish themselves from and not mimic "the Magians"; "...the pagans"; "...the Christians and the Jews."

Likewise, the Quran addresses the Prophet, *We have set you upon a sacred Law in this affair. So consistently adhere to it, and do not follow the vain desires of those who are devoid of knowledge.*[24] In the same light, the Prophet said, "Whoever imitates a people becomes one of them."[25]

Other forms of praiseworthy diversity in which Muslims should be distinct from non-Muslims are in the celebration of pagan sacred festivals and customary social practices, dress, and other commonly distinguishing factors that conflict with Islam.

Ibn Taymîyya, however, does hold the following noteworthy position:

> If a Muslim resides in a non-Muslim land that is either at war or peace [with Muslims], he is not compelled to oppose them in outward conduct because of the harm it may bring. In fact, it may be preferable or even mandatory for him to occasionally participate in their outward conduct provided that there is a religious benefit, such as inviting them to religion, repelling their harms from Muslims, or other virtuous ends.[26]

Acceptable differences in law may occur due to the variant opinions among judicial authorities (*mujtahids*) and jurists in matters lacking specific rulings by decisive Sharî'a Texts, thus making them liable to differing legal opinions. Consistent with this is the Prophet's statement reported in Bukhârî, "When a legitimate authority renders a correct judgment, he will enjoy double reward. But if he makes a mistake in judgment, he will be rewarded only once."[27] The Prophet's statement is explicit in acknowledging the possibility of a jurist making an error while confirming his reward, provided that deliberate misjudgment is ruled out.

Also in line with this are the known and tolerated differing opinions that existed among the Companions in the time of the Prophet, their Successors, and the imams and jurists of the legal schools after them.

Summary

• For legal differences to be valid, the conflicting opinions must issue from qualified jurists or *mujtahids*, who besides having thorough knowledge of Sharî'a Law must possess the insight and experience necessary to consider a people's unique conditions and circumstances. Commenting on the *fiqhî* differences that occurred in the first generation, Ibn Ḥazm states, "Blame should not be attributed to the Prophet's Companions with regard to their disputes. For they sought truth and strove to attain it. As such, they are rewarded."[28]

- Acceptable juristic diversity requires, along with sincere intention, avoidance of senseless argumentation and vanity.

PART TWO

THE CAUSES

I. Why Differences?

Although it is true that differences among people, no matter how subtle, are part of life, they should not become a *way* of life. It is important to reflect on why differences arise in earnest scholarship over matters of interpretation and opinion.

In general, depth and range of awareness often account for disagreements among those with common knowledge of Islam. "Dispute in my Ummah is a mercy," for instance, is a statement widely attributed to the Prophet in public circles. But it is not an authentic *ḥadîth*, as has been pointed out by many authorities.[29] Therefore, it cannot be used to support erroneous claims that *every opinion is right!*

This, however, raises another question: Is it possible that all the various legal opinions of qualified scholars are correct? Or is it the case that there are mistaken *and* correct ones? An interesting dialogue has developed among the jurists around this issue, some holding that all conflicting judgments are accurate. Al-Qarâfî, for instance, is reported to have described the relationship between legal variants qualitatively. He preferred the distinctions "more accurate" or "less accurate" and "further from the mark" or "nearer," arguing that the Sharî'a encompasses all decisions due to its great breadth.

The majority of legal theorists, however, believe that the truth of any given case is but one, though all jurists may not conclusively arrive at the correct position. However, the *mujtahid* who has fully and conscientiously exhausted his ability and missed the correct position does not commit a violation and is not blameworthy. On the contrary, he receives heavenly praise, as the Prophet, peace be upon him, stated; and people are free to follow these legitimate legal positions.

II. Causes of Legal Diversification

Close examination of Sharî'a Texts and juristic literature yields five principal causes for *khilâf*.

A. *The nature of the Arabic language—including the accurately preserved variant recitations of the Quran.*

B. *Differing methods of analysis and legal approaches among jurists.*

C. *Unfamiliarity or uncertainty regarding specific ḥadîth.*

D. *Apparent conflict between texts.*

E. *Unprecedented occurrences and issues not addressed specifically in the Sharî'a Texts and sources.*

Each of these aspects requires brief discussion.

A. The nature of Arabic

First, Arabic, as is known, is the language of Allah's Book and His Prophet. The variant (namely 'the seven') recitations of the Quran are accurately preserved and inexceptionably transmitted by an overwhelming number of reporters and reciters from, and on the authority of, the Prophet, upon him be peace.

Like other languages, Arabic has its native intricacies. Scholars have identified one such subtlety as *ishtirâk* or 'linguistic ambiguity,' meaning that some terms and phrases validly accept more than one meaning, where the alternate meaning is more literal and not merely a figurative nuance, as in the following examples.

- *'As'as* means both *advance* and *retreat*.
- *'Ayn* refers to the organ of sight (the eye), the metal gold, a wellspring, and also a thing's essence.
- *Qur'* means purity as well as menstruation.
- *Maḥîḍ* signifies menstruation or the female anatomical site of the conjugal act.

The Quran makes use of some of this equivocal terminology. As such, scholars differ in their comprehension of what exactly is meant by a given Text or context. Some prefer one possible meaning over another, while others choose the alternate.

The question of a man's engaging in non-conjugal intimacy with his wife during her menstruation period is a classic example of the kind of linguistic ambiguity that has led to different interpretations. *They seek guidance in regard to menstruation. Say it is a harm*, the Quran reads. Also, *Refrain from your women during menstruation. Do not approach them until they have purified themselves.*[30]

Regarding this verse, jurists differed in opinion because of the ambiguity of the term *maḥîḍ*, and its ability to accept more than one meaning.

What is meant by *do not approach them* during menstruation? Prominent jurists, such as Mâlik and Abû Ḥanîfa, and a large number of other scholars, concluded that the verse commands men to refrain from sexual intercourse with their wives during menstruation, except as had been clearly laid out in a *ḥadîth* reported by the Prophet's wife, 'A'isha. She stated that whenever the Prophet wanted to have direct physical contact with his wife during even the height of her menses, he would ask her to don a cloth before touching her.[31]

Shâfi'î (the second century namesake of the Shâfi'î school), in one opinion recorded of him, the jurists al-Thawrî, Dâwûd (both of the Ẓâhirî school), and Muḥammad b. al-Ḥasan (a Ḥanafî jurist), interpret the command *Refrain from your women during menstruation* to mean avoidance of the organ itself, that is, the place of menstruation.

Supporting this position are the well-known statements of the Prophet, in which it is recorded that the Jews altogether avoided their women during menstruation, neither sharing meals nor normal home-life with them. The Prophet was asked by his Companions as to the correctness of this practice. This occasioned Allah's revealing, *They ask you in regard to menstruation. . .* Hence, the Prophet then instructed his Companions, "Tell them they may do everything except intercourse."[32]

Another significant cause of juristic divergence when it comes to language is the various *Quranic recitations* approved by the Prophet. A good example is the Quranic verse referring to the washing of the feet in ritual ablution (*wuḍû'*). Does it state that we are obliged to 'wash' them or will a symbolic 'passing' of the hands over them suffice?

The underlying cause of the different opinions is the possible readings of the verse, *When you stand to pray, wash your faces, and hands to the elbows, then wipe your heads, and feet to the ankles.*[33]

The discussion hinges on a point of Arabic grammar. The reading of the scholars 'Âṣim, Nâfi', Ibn 'Amr, and Kisâ'î renders the word for 'feet' as *arjul͟akum* (accusative). Others, like Ibn Kathîr, Abû 'Amr, and Ḥamza recited the same word as *arjuli̱kum* (genitive). This variation in recitation gives way to divergence in law.

In accepting the first reading, *arjulakum*, where 'feet' becomes the object of 'wash,' not 'wipe,' scholars commit to the position that *washing* of the feet is obliged. There is support for this in the Prophet's practice. Jurists cite a *ḥadîth* of the Prophet that establishes the obligation of washing the feet during ablution. 'Abdullah b. 'Amr b. al-'Âṣ reports as recorded in Bukhârî and Muslim, "We parted from the Prophet in one of his trips. Then he caught up with us when we were pressed by time for the late afternoon prayer. So we began making ablution, and wiping our feet, whereupon the Prophet called out in his loudest voice, 'Woe to the heels from the fire [if they are not washed].' He said it two or three times."[34]

The practice of the Prophet strengthens the statements recorded of him. He regularly washed his feet for prayer if he was barefooted, and wiped over his footwear if in shoes or leather socks.

This is the opinion of most scholars—the stronger one according to Sunni juristic literature, in terms of evidence and validity. Also, while the common recitation in the Quran is *arjuli̱kum* (genitive), the term's inflection is more reflective of word order, thus restricting the command 'wipe' to the object 'heads.'

In support of this linguistic interpretation, jurists cite the following lines from an Arab poet:

I fed her straw and water cold
Until her eyes poured tears

It is clear that the person *fed* the animal straw and *gave* her cold water to drink. Linguistic convention accepts this usage.

In this regard, it should be said that the rules of

Arabic grammar in the Quran do not in and of themselves necessitate rulings of *fiqh*. There are, however, some juristic schools, among them the Ja'farî Shî'a, who argue that one is obliged only to wipe his or her feet during ablution and not wash them. This opinion has been attributed to Ibn 'Abbâs and other Companions and their Successors.

One may also add the view of the literalist, who looks at this same verse and, since it contains two meanings, says the obligation is both *washing* and *wiping*. Others yet, like Ibn Jarîr al-Ṭabarî (d. 310/923), see it as a choice between *washing* and *wiping*.

The jurist Muḥammad b. 'Alî al-Shawkânî (d. 1834 C.E.), on the other hand, saw no ambiguity and said: "As for those who have made *wiping* mandatory, they have not presented clear, decisive proof. Moreover they differ [in effect] from the Quran and [in fact] from the consensus in the *ḥadîth* literature."[35]

B. Differing methods of analysis & legal approaches

The second basic causal factor for *khilâf* is how a jurist approaches an issue and to what extent he interprets a Text. This is primarily a matter of method. Therefore, an important consideration here is simply what sources a jurist accepts as valid, aside from the Quran and Sunna. The two most prominent are *qiyâs*, proof by analogy, and *ijmâ'*, proof by consensus.

As for ***qiyâs***, the Ḥanafîs, for instance, are known to give much weight to 'reasoning' in their method. They use proof by analogy, *qiyâs*, extensively, holding it as a significant 'source' for arriving at Sharî'a rulings. In other words, when they face an unprecedented case, they apply, through analogy, the relevant Islamic rule that has precedent in the Quran or Sunna.

But while the Ḥanafîs rely heavily on *qiyâs*—and indeed rebuff those who reject its use—other jurists disallow it as a *source* of Sharî'a. Indeed, some discredit its use completely. It is easy to see how such a difference in method can lead to juristic differences.

When it comes to ***ijmâ'***, or consensus, most schools accept its validity as a source of law but differ on how it may be constituted. *Ijmâ'*, in general, is the consensus of the Ummah (Community) or its recognized scholars. The Mâlikîs readily acknowledge consensus as a valid source, but limit the legitimacy of consensus to the community of Madinah—the city of the Prophet—in the earlier Muslim centuries.

The Shâfi'îs, on the other hand, reject limiting consensus to Madinah, saying it is all Muslims at any given time, as represented by the community of scholars. Others have held—though practically it is impossible—that consensus can only be established by all Muslims from day one until the end of time, which means there could not be *ijmâ'* until the Day of Judgement.

These differences in methodology can profoundly affect the juristic conclusions of various schools. The following case involving *qiyâs* further clarifies this point.

The Ẓâhirî school, known for its literalist interpretations, refuses analogy as a Sharî'a principle. So their jurists conclude, for instance, that deliberate eating or drinking during the fast of Ramadan does not necessitate atonement, or *kaffâra*. They reason that *kaffâra* is necessary only for intercourse between husband and wife during the fast of Ramadan as based on a statement of the Prophet specifically indicating such. But since a valid *ḥadîth* addressed the violation of the fast by way of intercourse and did not explicitly specify deliberate eating or drinking during the fast, these latter acts—though they violate fasting—do not necessitate atonement.[36]

The majority of jurists, however, extend the ruling, by way of analogy, to include deliberate eating or drinking during Ramadan based on this *ḥadîth*. Therefore, they considered atonement as obligatory for those who break their fast by either eating or drinking, as it is with marital intercourse, during the prescribed daily fasts.

In another example, a number of reports related to the Prophet indicate that it is permissible to say the *iqâma* (the second call to prayer telling worshippers prayer is imminent) by repeating each phrase twice rather than once, exactly as is done in the *adhân* (the first call indicating that the time for prayer has arrived.)

Yet Mâlik disagreed with this understanding based on the fact that the practice of the Madinah community was contrary to it. He considered consensus, *ijmâ'*, a Sharî'a source, but limited it to the consensus of the scholars of Madinah. "As for the *iqâma*, its phrases cannot be repeated [like the *adhân*]," he says in his book *al-Muwaṭṭa*, adding that "this, in fact, is the practice of the scholars in our city [Madinah]."[37]

There are many case studies showing the effect of juristic method on Sharî'a rulings. Analyzing them helps one understand the differing viewpoints of the various schools of thought.

C. Unfamiliarity or uncertainty regarding specific ḥadîth

Third of the five causes for legal divergence is a jurist's lack of familiarity with a *ḥadîth*, or doubt of its authenticity.

Needless to say, incomplete knowledge or doubt about the Quran cannot be used as a reason to justify dispute. This is because the Quran has been reported through what is called *tawâtur*, a consecutive, overwhelming, inexceptionable chain of reporters. Thus unfamiliarity with a Quranic Text, unlike a particular *ḥadîth*, is not justifiable.

Muslim scholars recognize that not all *ḥadîth* have been reported through *tawâtur* from the Messenger of Allah. No one should find it strange that a number of jurists—even among the Companions—were unaware of some *ḥadîths*, either forgetting them or simply not knowing that the Prophet had said them. Abû Bakr, the first Caliph, for instance, did not know the Prophet's ruling on the share of the grandmother's inheritance. He sought the answer from various Companions until he found it with al-Mughîra b. Shu'ba and Muḥammad b. Maslama. Both reported the Prophet's ruling in this case.

Also, Abû Hurayra, the Companion whose name has become synonymous with the narration of *ḥadîth*, used to say, "Whosoever wakes up after dawn during Ramadan in a state of *janâba* [ritual impurity after sexual relations], his fasting is invalid." He was not aware of the authentic report by the Prophet's wife, 'Â'isha, that the Prophet sometimes heard the *adhân* for dawn prayer while in the state of *janâba*. Yet he continued his fast.[38]

Again, 'Abdullah b. 'Amr b. al-'Âs used to instruct women who performed ritual bathing, *ghusl*, after either completing menstruation or giving birth, to unbraid or comb out their hair. 'Â'isha objected to this saying, as only she could, "What a strange position from the son of 'Amr. Shouldn't he require them also to shave their heads? When I use to perform *ghusl* with the Prophet from a single vessel, I simply poured water on my head three times."[39]

Other examples showing that some jurists were either unaware of a *ḥadîth* or doubtful about it are found in Bukhârî and Muslim. In a story involving Abû Mûsâ al-Ash'arî, it is said he once approached a gathering of the Anṣâr, the indigenous residents of Madinah who accepted Islam, seeking corroboration from anyone who had heard the Prophet explaining the etiquette for taking permission to enter the residence of another. "Only the most junior of us who heard the Prophet should go with you," replied Ubay b. Ka'b. So Abû Sa'îd al-Khudrî, in support of Abû Mûsâ's testimony, accompanied Abû Hurayra to 'Umar b. al-Khaṭṭâb, the second Caliph, who had apparently wanted to verify that more than one person had heard the Prophet explaining the etiquette of visitation. (The Messenger of Allah had said, "When any of you seeks permission three [consecutive] times to enter the residence of another [for example, knocking on the door or calling] and permission is not granted or an answer is not given, you must withdraw.")[40]

Understanding this cause of juristic difference and reflecting on it explains the occurrence of this phenomenon, even among the Companions and their Successors. Bear in mind that direct knowledge of the Prophet's teachings was attained by those who saw him and heard him. Each of them retained as much as he or she could without complete mastery over it all.

The Companions who traveled to various regions taught the Successors whatever they knew, who taught people after them, and so on, through the meticulous—and unparalleled—system of *riwâya*, transmission of *ḥadîth* from one generation to the next, until this day. Yet after the monumental and exhaustive efforts of our predecessors to report Sunna and record it in the various collections, it may not be an extreme position to say that ignorance of a *ḥadîth* in our time is no longer a justifiable excuse for any jurist making a judgement. "I do not know the *ḥadîth*," then, is inadequate; for virtually all of these *ḥadîth* Texts are available to us, and the task of the would-be jurist begins by educating him or herself about them.

D. Apparent Conflict between Texts

Fourth in the causes of *khilâf* is conflict between 'proofs.' It may sometimes appear that conflict exists between various Sharî'a Texts. Therefore, in acknowledging the validity of one proof over another, or in adopting one to the exclusion of others, jurists may differ based on their approach to the texts.

For example, the Prophet's *ḥadîth*, "Whosoever touches his genitals should not pray without performing ablution" is in apparent conflict with another in which the Prophet was asked about the incidental self-touching of one's genitals during prayer; he answered, "Isn't it part of your body?" clearly implying that the prayer should be completed.

The first *ḥadîth* is held by Shâfi'î and Isḥâq Ibn Râhuwayh[41] to be the latest statement of the Prophet in this matter. Therefore it would abrogate the other reports on this topic. But Ḥanafî jurists have adopted the second *ḥadîth* as valid, expressing uncertainty about the authenticity of the first. Clearly, the cause of difference is the apparent conflict between the two statements in reference to one particular case, while lacking any consensus indicating the precedence of one over the other.

E. Unprecedented Occurrences Not Specifically Addressed by the Sharî'a Texts.

The fifth basis for juristic difference is the absence of a specific Sharî'a Text addressing an unprecedented case.

There are abundant examples that illustrate this, such as the many issues and challenges facing the contemporary global Muslim community in the areas of finance, government, sociology, and other fields. The Sharî'a Texts leave room for juristic ingenuity to generate and specify needed Islamic rulings and positions—the basis of which remains, of course, on scholarly reliance on recognized sources of Law, foundational principles of the Sharî'a, and societal dynamics.

It should not be unexpected that juristic rulings and conclusions in these cases may differ based on the extent of individual knowledge and mastery of issues. Variance occurs naturally as new issues and cases emerge. But while the Sharî'a Texts are finite, the extent of the application of their principles, wisdom, and morals are infinite; Islam is the decreed way of life for humanity until the Day of Judgement. It is therefore incumbent upon every Muslim generation to find solutions for new issues. So today's jurists should not freeze in their tracks when faced with juristic challenges, claiming that there are no specific precedents to follow.

Rather, we have a relevant model in the Companions after the death of the Prophet. Many specific cases arose that did not emerge during his lifetime. Yet they faced them. For example, the governor of Yemen requested the Caliph 'Umar to render a judgement for an unprecedented crime. A man, his wife, their servant, and a friend together killed a young boy, dismembered him, stuffed him in a leather container, and threw him in an abandoned well. When 'Umar consulted with the Companions noted as jurists, many said all must be executed for killing the young boy. Others argued that the killing of one human soul does not justify the execution of more than one person.

Ultimately, 'Umar sanctioned the execution of all accomplices to the boy's murder, saying that were the entire community of Ṣan'â, the capital of Yemen, found in complicity with the slaying, all should be executed. 'Alî b. Abî Ṭâlib, among others, supported 'Umar in this position.

In this way the Sharî'a remains a wellspring of justice, keeping revealed Law evergreen for those who desire to live within the encompassing unity of Allah's justice on earth.

CONCLUSION

This primer on juristic dispute is a window to this important aspect of the world of Islamic Law. It does not teach *fiqh*, per se, or its sources, but the main causes and principles of juristic variance. This work is not aimed merely at providing information, but at helping introduce a new attitude and fresh way of thinking about the world of differing.

In this direction, it is hoped that we can agree on the following 'heart-set':

- Whosoever accepts the true *tawḥîd*, Allah's Oneness, expressed in the Quran and Sunna, is a brother or a sister to every Muslim and *must* be loved and accorded loyalty and support based on the integrity of that commitment. And those who choose not to accept Islam have the right to be introduced to the Quran and its Sharî'a in the most gentle way, being secure in life, wealth, and, most importantly, dignity.
- The principal Muslim references are the Book of

Allah and the Sunna of His Messenger. Their interpretation must be based on the original Arabic texts, free from bias and contrived meanings.

• If qualified, legitimately chosen leaders in a given Muslim community or association see fit to adopt certain juristic positions for the general welfare of the community, or give valid preference to some opinions over others, it is essential for the members to honor these positions. But blind loyalty to one person or a particular juristic school is not befitting of any Muslim. The Sharî'a recognizes the wisdom of following juristic authorities; yet *know* the basis of their judgements and approach them with an open mind for guidance or correction—even if they differ with one's own bias or juristic affiliation.

• All that has been reported to us from preceding generations (in harmony with the Book of Allah and the Sunna of the Prophet) is accepted with awareness of the context involved. Insult, accusation, and innuendo are beneath the dignity of a Muslim. *This is a community that has passed on. For them is what they have earned. For you is what you have earned. And you will not be questioned about what they have done.*[42]

Bear this in heart: *Fiqhî* dispute is forbidden if it leads to fighting, hatred, and fragmentation in the community, involving it in endless and senseless argumentation and disagreement. Cooperation in areas of agreement, toleration for others, and understanding another's point of view must be our attitude. Ḥasan al-

Banna frequently said, "We cooperate in whatever we agree upon. And let us excuse one another in the areas where we disagree."[43] I would go further in urging the intelligent exchange of views—even contrary ones—and advice on how to minimize contention.

Let our position toward *fiqhî* differences regarding the details of the Sharî'a go only this far: "Our founded opinion is correct, but liable to misjudgment; differing opinions are misjudgments, but plausibly correct."

We ask Allah to honor us with devotion to His service and the ability to distinguish right from wrong. Indeed, Allah guides whom He wills to the straight way. In the end, as in the beginning, all praise belongs to Allah, the Lord of the worlds.

ENDNOTES

[1]Ignaz Goldziher, "Catholic Tendencies in Islam," translated from "Katholische Tendenz und Partikularismus im Islam" by Merlin Swartz, *Studies on Islam* (New York: Oxford University Press, 1981), p.123.

[2]Al-Râghib al-Aṣfahânî, *al-Mufradât* (Beirut: Dâr al-Fikr, 1972), p. 156. His full name is al-Ḥusayn b. Muḥammad b. al-Mufaḍḍal (Abû al-Qâsim al-Aṣfahânî, d. 502/1108). He is among the most highly regarded men of letters in Islamic history, having lived in Baghdad in the 5th Islamic century as a contemporary of the great Abû Ḥâmid al-Ghazâlî. He wrote widely in fields as varied as literature, linguistics, rhetoric, Sharî'a, Quranic exegesis, and psychology.

[3]Quran, Sûrat Maryam, 19:37.

[4]Ibrâhîm b. Mûsâ b. Muḥammad al-Lakhmî al-Ghurnâṭî [Abû Isḥâq al-Shâṭibî], *al-Muwâfaqât fî Uṣûl al-Fiqh*, 4 vols. (Beirut: Dâr al-Ma'rifa, n.d), 4:222. Al-Shâṭibî (d. 739/1338), who lived in Grenada, Spain, was a towering jurist of the Mâlikî school and a scholar of the principles of Islamic Law. His works are highly regarded and often consulted to this day.

[5]Quran, Sûrat Âl 'Imrân, 3:103.

[6]Quran, Sûrat al-Ṣaff, 61:4.

[7]Quran, Sûrat al-Anfâl, 8:46.

[8]Quran, Sûrat Âl 'Imrân, 3:105.

[9]Ahmad Ibn Ḥajar al-'Asqalânî, *Fatḥ al-Bârî bi Sharḥ Ṣaḥîḥ al-Bukhârî*, 13 vols. (Maktabat al-Riyâḍ al-Ḥadîtha, nd), 9:101.

[10]Ismâ'îl al-'Ajlûnî, *Kashf al-Khafâ' wa Muzîl al-Ilbâs 'amma Ashtahara min al-Aḥâdîth 'alâ Alsinat al-Nâs,* 2 vols. ed. Aḥmad al-Qalâs (Beruit: Mu'assasat al-Risâla, n.d.), 2:529.

[11]Quran, Sûrat al-Nûr, 24:63.

[12]Quran, Sûrat al-Mujâdila, 58:20.

[13]Quran, Sûrat al-Baqara, 2:286.

[14]Quran, Sûrat Âl 'Imrân, 3:105.

[15]Quran, Sûrat Âl 'Imrân, 3:190.

[16]Quran, Sûrat al-Rûm, 30:2.

[17]Quran, Sûrat Hûd, 11:118.

[18]Aḥmad b. Ḥanbal, *al-Musnad* (Beirut: al-Maktab al-Islâmî: 1969), 2:332.

[19]Ibn Ḥajar al-'Asqalânî, *Fatḥ al-Bârî,* 13:536.

[20]Muḥammad b. Yaḥya b. 'Abdullâh Abû Bakr al-Sûlî b. Lubâba was also one of the great scholars of literature in Muslim Spain (d. 330/942). See Abû Faḍl 'Iyâḍ's *Tartîb al-Madârik wa Taqrîb al-Masâlik li Ma'rifat A'lâm Madhhab Mâlik,* 4 vols. edited by Aḥmad b. Maḥmûd (Beirut: Maktabat al-Ḥayât, 1967), 4:398-403.

[21]See Khayr al-Dîn al-Ziriklî, *al-A'lâm Qâmûs Tarâjum,* 8 vols. (Beirut: Dâr al-'Ilm li al-Malâyîn, 1980), 3:324.

[22]*Waqf*, in general, is any money, property, or other asset specifically dedicated for religious use or service. Once declared as *waqf*, the asset is considered a sacred endowment that cannot be violated without proper cause.

[23]Abû Isḥâq Shâṭibî, *al-Muwâfaqât*, 4 vols. edited by 'Abd Allâh Drâz (Beirut: Dâr al-Ma'rifa, n.d.), 4:37-38. See also See Abû Faḍl 'Iyâḍ's *Tartîb al-Madârik*, 4:401-402.

[24]Quran, Sûrat al-Jâthiyah, 45:18.

[25]Aḥmad b. Ḥanbal, *al-Musnad*, 2:50.

[26]Aḥmad Ibn Taymîyya, *Iqtiḍâ'al-Ṣirâṭ al-Mustaqîm Mukhâlafat Aṣḥâba al-Jaḥîm,* 2 vols. (Cairo: Dâr Anṣâr al-Sunna al-Muḥammadiyya), pp. 176-177.

[27]Ibn Ḥajar al-'Asqalânî, *Fatḥ al-Bârî,* 13:317-320. Also see A. J. Wensinck, *Concordance et Indices de la Traditione Musulmane,* 7 vols. (Leiden: E.J. Brill, 1936-1969), 1:390.

[28]'Alî b. 'Umar b. Ḥazm, *Uṣûl al-Aḥkâm*, 8 vols., ed. Aḥmad Muḥammad Shâkir (Cairo: Maktabat al-Khanjî, 1926-1928), p. 645.

[29]Shaykh Muḥammad Nâṣir al-Dîn al-Albânî, in his *Silsilat al-Aḥâdîth al-Ḍa'îfa wa al-Mawḍû'a*, 4th edition (Beruit: Al-Maktab al-Islâmî, 1978), 1:76-78, has an elaborate discussion on the unauthenticity of this *ḥadîth* where he cites Ibn Ḥazm and other sources.

[30]Quran, Sûrat al-Baqara, 2:222.

[31]Abû Dawûd, *Sunan*, 4 vols. (Cairo: Sa'âda Press, 1935, reprinted by Dâr al-Fikr, Damascus), 1:171.

[32]See Wahba al-Zahîlî, *al-Fiqh al-Islâmî wa Adillatuh*, 2nd ed. 8 vols. (Damascus: Dâr al-Fikr,1985), 1:473.

[33]Quran, Sûrat al-Mâ'ida, 5:6.

[34]*Ṣaḥîḥ Muslim*, #240, 1:213-215. See also al-Zaḥîlî, *al-Fiqh al-Islâmî wa Adillatuh*, 1:223.

[35]Muḥammad b. 'Alî al-Shawkânî, *Nayl al-Awṭâr*, 9 vols. (Beirut: Dâr al-Jîl, 1973), 1:168.

[36]*Ṣaḥîḥ Bukhârî*, #1936.

[37]Mâlik b. Anas, *al-Muwaṭṭa'*, 2 vols. ed. Muḥammad 'Abd al-Bâqî (n.p.: Dâr al-Turâth al-'Arabî, n.d.), 1:71.

[38]*Ṣaḥîḥ Muslim*, #1109, 2:779.

[39]*Ṣaḥîḥ Muslim*, #319, 1:255.

[40]*Ṣaḥîḥ Muslim*, #2153, 3:1694-1697.

[41]Ibn Râhuwayh (d. 238/853) was a great scholar of *ḥadîth*. In fact he served as an important source for the well-known collectors of *ḥadîth* literature, such as al-Bukhârî, Muslim, Aḥmad b. Ḥanbal, and others. Ibn Râhuwayh was known for his travels throughout the Muslim world in quest of knowledge and scholarship.

[42]Quran, Sûrat al-Baqara, 2:134.

[43]*Al-Uṣûl al-'Ishrûn*, by Ḥasan al-Banna.

BIBLIOGRAPHY

'Abd al-Bâqî, M. Fu'âd. *Al-Mu'jam al-Mufahras li Alfâẓ al-Qur'ân al-Karîm.* Cairo, 1378 H.

Abû al-Baqâ' al-Ḥusaynî al-Kaffawî. *Kullîyât.* 4 vols. Damascus, 1974.

Abû Dâwûd. *Sunan.* 4 vols. Cairo: Sa'âda Press, 1935 (Reprinted by Dâr al-Fikr, Damascus).

Abû Zahrah, Muḥammad. *Abû Ḥanîfah: Ḥayâtuhu wa 'Asruhu wa Âthâruhu wa Fiqhuhu.* Cairo: Dâr al-Fikr al-'Arabî, n.d.

____. *Mâlik: Ḥayâtuhu wa 'Asruhu wa Âthâruhu wa Fiqhuhu.* Cairo: Dâr al-Fikr al-'Arabî, n.d.

____. *Târîkh al-Madhâhib al-Islâmîyya.* Cairo: Dâr al-Fikr al-'Arabî, n.d.

____. *Uṣûl al-Fiqh.* Cairo: Dâr al-Fikr al-'Arabî, n.d.

al-'Ajlûnî, Ismâ'îl. *Kashf al-Khafâ' wa Muzîl al-Ilbâs 'amma Ashtahara min al-Aḥâdîth 'alâ Alsinat al-Nâs.* 2 vols. Ed. Aḥmad al-Qalâs. Beruit: Mu'assasat al-Risâla, n.d.

al-Âmidî, Ṣayf al-Dîn. *Al-Iḥkâm fî Uṣûl al-Aḥkâm.* 4 vols. Beirut: Dâr al-Kutub al-'Ilmîyya, 1980.

____. *Al-Iḥkâm fî Uṣûl al-Aḥkâm.* 4 vols. Edited by Sayyid al-Jumaylî. Beirut: Dâr al-Kitâb al-'Arabî, 1984.

al-Anṣârî, 'Abd al-A'lâ Muḥammad. *Fawâtiḥ al-Raḥamût bi Sharḥ Musallam al-Thubût.* (Printed with *al-Mustaṣfâ*) 2 vols. Baghdâd: Maktabat al-Mathannâ, 1970.

A'ẓamî, Muḥammad Muṣṭafâ. *Dirâsât fî al-Ḥadîth al-Nabawî.* 2vols. Beruit: Al-Maktab al-Islâmî, 1980.

Badrân, Abû al-'Aynayn. *Uṣûl al-Aḥkâm al-Fiqh al-Islâmî.* Mu'assasat

Shabâb al-Jâmi'a, 1984.

al-Baghdâdî, al-Khaṭîb. *Kitâb al-Faqîh wa al-Mutafaqqih.* 2 vols. 2nd ed. Edited by Ismâ'îl al-Anṣârî. Beirut: Dâr al-Kutub al-'Ilmîyya, 1980.

al-Baghdâdî, Ṣayf al-Dîn 'Abd al-Mu'min b. 'Abd al-Ḥaqq. *Marâṣid al-Aṭla'.* 3 vols. Edited by 'Alî al-Bijâwî. Beirut: Dâr al-Ma'rifa, 1954.

al-Bâjî, Abû al-Walîd. *Kitâb al-Ḥudûd fî al-Uṣûl.* Edited by Nazîh Ḥammad. Beirut: Mu'assasa al-Za'bi, 1973.

____. Al-*Muntaqa: Sharḥ Muwaṭṭa' al-Imâm Mâlik.* 6 vols. Cairo: Maṭba'at al-Sa'âda, 1332 A.H.; reprint ed., Beirut: Dâr al-Kitâb al-'Arabî, n.d.

al-Bânî, M. Sa'îd. *'Umdât al-Taḥqîq.* Beirut: Al-Maktab al-Islâmî, 1981.

al-Bayanûnî, Muḥammad. *Dirasât fî al-Ikhtilâfât al-Fiqhîyya.* Ḥalab: Maktabat al-Hudâ, n.d.

al-Bughâ, Muṣṭafâ Dîb. *Athar al-Adillah al-Mukhtalaf fîhâ fî al-Fiqh al-Islâmî.* Dâr al-Imâm al-Bukhârî, n.d.

al-Bukhârî, 'Abd al-'Azîz. *Kashf al-Asrâr 'alâ Uṣûl al-Pazdawî* (also *Bazdawî*). 4 vols. Edited by Aḥmad Râmiz. n.p.: Ḥasan Ḥilmî al-Rayzawî, 1307 A.H.

al-Bukhârî, Muḥammad b. Ismâ'îl. *Ṣaḥîḥ.* 12 vols. Edited by 'Abd al-Azîz b. Bâz and M. Fu'âd 'Abd al-Bâqî. Cairo: Al-Maktaba al-Salafîyya, n.d.

al-Bûṭî, Muḥammad Ramaḍân. *Ḍawâbiṭ al-Maṣlaḥa fî al-Sharî'a al-Islâmîyya.* Beirut: Mu'assisat al-Risâla, n.d.

al-Dabbûsî, Abû Zayd 'Ubayd-Allâh. *Ta'sîs al-Naẓar.* Edited by Zakarîya 'Alî Yûsuf. Cairo: Imâm's Press, 1972.

_____. *Taqwîm Uṣûl al-Fiqh wa Taḥdîd Adillat al-Shar'.* Cairo, Dâr al-Kutub, MMS, 255.

al-Dhahabî, Muḥammad b. Aḥmad. *Kitâb al-Mushtabih fî al-Rijâl: Asmâ'ihim wa Ansâbihim.* 2 vols. Beruit, 1962.

al-Farrâ', Abû Ya'la. *Al-'Udda fî Uṣûl al-Fiqh.* Edited by Aḥmad b. 'Alî al-Mubârakî. 3 vols. Beirut: Mu'assasat al-Risâla, 1980.

al-Fârûqî, Ḥârith Sulaymân. *Fârûqî's Law Dictionary: English-Arabic*

3d. revised edition. Beirut: Librairie du Liban, 1980.

al-Ghazâlî, Abû Ḥâmid Muḥammad. *Al-Mankhûl min Ta'liqât al-Uṣûl.* Edited by Muḥammad H. Haytu. Beirut: Dar al-Fikr, n.d.

____. *Al-Mustaṣfâ min 'Ilm al-Uṣûl.* 2 vols. Bulâq, Egypt: Amîrîyya Press, 1322-24/1905-7.

____. *Shifâ' al-Ghalîl fî Bayân al-Shabah wa al-Mukhîl wa Masâlik al-Ta'lîl.* Edited by Ḥamad al-Kubaysî. Baghdad: Maṭba'at al-Irshâd, 1390/1971.

Goldziher, Ignaz. *Introduction to Islamic Theology and Law.* Translated by Andras & Ruth Hamori. Princeton: Princeton University Press, 1981.

____. *The Zahirites: Their Doctrine and their History.* Translated by Wolfgang Behn. Leiden: E.J. Brill, 1971.

al-Ḥâkim, Muḥammad b. 'Abdullah al-Nîsâbûrî. *Al-Mustadrak.* 4 vols. Hyderabad: n.p., 1334 H.

Ḥasaballâh, 'Alî. *Uṣûl al-Tashrî' al-Islâmî.* Cairo: Dâr al-Ma'ârif, 1971.

Ḥasan, Aḥmad. *The Doctrine of Ijmâ' in Islam: A Study of the Juridical Principle of Consensus.* Islamabad: Islamic Research Institute, 1978.

Ḥassân, Ḥusayn Ḥâmid. *Al-Ḥukm al-Shar'î 'inda al-Uṣûlîyyîn.* Cairo: Dâr al-Nahḍa al-'Arabîyya, 1972.

____. *Al-Madkhal li Dirâsat al-Fiqh al-Islâmî.* Cairo: Dâr al-Nahḍa al-'Arabîyya, 1972.

____. *Uṣûl al-Fiqh.* Cairo: Dâr al-Nahḍa al-'Arabîyya,1970.

al-Ḥijwî, Muḥammad. *Al-Fikr al-Sâmî fî Târîkh al-Fiqh al-Islâmî.* 2 vols. Edited by A. al-Qârî. Madina: Al-Maktaba al-'Ilmîyya, 1977.

al-Ḥimayrî, 'Abd al-Mun'im. *Kitâb al-Rawḍ al-Mi'ṭar fî Khabar al-Aqṭâr.* Edited by Iḥsân 'Abbâs. Beirut: Library of Lebanon, 1975.

al-Ḥimyarî, Sa'îd 'Alî Muḥammad. *Al-Ḥukm al-Waḍ'î 'ind al-Uṣûlîyyîn.* Makka: Al-Fayṣalîyya, 1404/1984.

Hîtû, Muḥammad Ḥasan. *Al-Wajîz fî Uṣûl al-Tashrî' al-Islâmî.* Beirut: Mu'assasat al-Risâla,1983.

Ibn 'Abd al-Salâm, 'Izz al-Dîn. *Qawâ'id al-Aḥkâm fî Maṣâliḥ al-Anâm.* 2 vols. Edited by Ṭâha A. Sa'd. Beirut: Dâr al-Jîl, 1980.

Ibn al-Amîr al-Ḥâjj. *Al-Taqrîr wa al-Taḥbîr.* 3 vols. Egypt: Amîrî Press, 1316-1318 H.

Ibn Badrân, 'Abd al-Qâdir b. Aḥmad. *Al-Madkhal ilâ Madhhab al-Imâm Aḥmad b. Ḥanbal.* 2d ed. Damascus: Dâr Iḥyâ' al-Turâth al-'Arabî, 1981.

_____. *Nuzhat al-Khâṭir al-'Aṭir Sharḥ Rawḍat al-Nâẓir wa Junnat al-Munâẓir.* 3 vols. Beirut: Dâr al-Kutub al-'Ilmîyya, n.d.

Ibn Ḥajar al-'Asqalânî, Aḥmad. *Al-Durar al-Kâminah fî A'yân al-Mi'ah al-Thâminah.* Hyderabad, 1348-50.

____. *Fatḥ al-Bârî bî Sharḥ Ṣaḥîḥ al-Bukhârî.* 13 vols. Maktabt al-Riyâḍ al-Ḥadîtha, nd.

_____. *Lisân al-Mizân.* 7 vols. 2nd ed. Beruit: Mu'assasat al-A'lamî li al-Maṭbu'ât, 1390/1971.

____. *Tabṣîr al-Muntabih bi Taḥrîr al-Mushtabih.* Edited by 'Alî Muḥammad al-Bajâwî Cairo: The Egyptian Organization for Authorship and Translation, 1965.

_____. *Tahdhîb al-Tahdhîb.* Beirut: Dâr al-Fikr, 1985.

Ibn Ḥanbal, Aḥmad. *Al-Musnad*, Beirut: Al-Maktab al-Islâmî: 1969.

Ibn Ḥazm, 'Alî b. Aḥmad. *Al-Iḥkâm fî Uṣûl al-Aḥkâm.* 8 vols. (in two). Edited by Aḥmad Muḥammad Shâkir. Cairo: Maktabat al-Khanjî,1926-1928.

_____. *Marâtib al-Ijmâ'.* (Published with *Naqḍ Marâtib al-Ijmâ'* by Ibn Taymîyya) 2nd ed. Beirut: Dâr al-Âfâq al-Jadîda, 1980.

_____. *Mulakhkhaṣ Ibṭâl al-Qiyâs wa al-Ra'y wa al-Istiḥsân wa al-Taqlîd wa al-Ta'lîl.* Damascus: Jâmi'a Damashq, 1379/1960.

Ibn al-Humâm, Kamâl al-Dîn Muḥammad. *Sharḥ Fatḥ al-Qadîr.* Beirut: Dâr Ṣâdir, n.d.

_____. *Al-Taḥrîr fî Uṣûl al-Fiqh al-Jâmi' bayn Iṣṭilâḥay al-Ḥanafîyyah wa al-Shâfi'îyyah.* Cairo: Muṣṭafâ al-Bâbî al-Ḥalabî wa Awlâduhu, 1351 H.

Ibn Khaldûn, 'Abd al-Raḥmân. *The Muqaddimah: An Introduction to*

History. Trans. by Franz Rosenthal. 3 vols. Princeton: Princeton University Press, 1967.

Ibn Mâjah, Muḥammad. b. Yazîd. *Al-Sunan*. 2 vols. Edited by M. Fu'âd 'Abd al-Bâqî. Cairo: 'Isâ al-Bâbî al-Ḥalabî, 1952.

Ibn Manẓûr, Abû al-Faḍl Jamâl al-Dîn b. Mukarram. *Lisân al-'Arab*. 15 vols. Cairo: Dâr Ṣâdir, n.d.

Ibn al-Qayyim al-Jawzîyyah, Shams al-Din Muḥammad. *I'lâm al-Muwaqqi'în*. 4 vols. Edited by Ṭâha A. Sa'd. Cairo: Maktabat al-Kullîyyât al-Azharîyyah, 1980.

____. *Zâd al-Ma'âd fî Hady Khayr al-'Ibâd*. Edited by Shu'ayb al-Arnâ'ut and 'Abd al-Qâdir al-Arnâ'ut. Beirut: Mu'assasat al-Risâla, 1979.

Ibn Qudâma, Muwaffaq al-Dîn. *Rawḍat al-Nâẓir wa Junnat al-Munâẓir fî Uṣûl al-Fiqh 'ala Madhhab al-Imâm Aḥmad b. Ḥanbal*. 2 vols. Beirut: Dâr al-Kutub al-'Ilmîyya, 1981.

Ibn Rushd, Abû al-Walîd. *Bidâyat al-Mujtahid wa Nihâyat al-Muqtaṣid*. 2 vols. Beirut: Dâr al-Fikr, n.d.

Ibn Taymîyya, Aḥmad b. 'Abd al-Halîm. *Majmu' al-Fatâwâ*. 39 vols. Rabat: Maktabat al-Ma'ârif, n.d.

Idlibî, Ṣalâḥ al-Dîn. *Manhaj Naqd al-Matn 'ind 'Ulamâ' al-Ḥadîth*. Beirut: Dâr al-Âfâq al-Jadîda, 1983.

al-Isnawî, Jamâl al-Dîn. *Nihâyat al-Uṣûl fî Sharḥ Minhâj al-Wuṣûl ilâ al-Uṣûl li al-Qâḍî al-Bayḍâwî*. 4 vols. Beirut: Al-Maṭba'at al-Salafîyya, 1982.

'Iyâḍ, Abû Faḍl b. Mûsâ al-Qâḍî. *Tartîb al-Madârik wa Taqrîb al-Masâlik li Ma'rifat A'lâm Madhhab Mâlik*. 4 vols. Edited by Aḥmad b. Maḥmûd. Beirut: Maktabat al-Ḥayât, 1967.

al-Jawharî, Ismâ'îl b. Ḥammâd. *Al-Ṣiḥâḥ*. 6 vols. Cairo, 1957; reprint, Beirut, 1979.

Kaḥḥâla, 'Umar Riḍâ. *Mu'jam al-Mu'allifîn: Tarâjum Muṣannafî al-Kutub al-'Arabîyya*. 15 vols. Beirut: Maktabat al-Muthannâ, 1957.

al-Kalwadhânî, Abû al-Khaṭṭâb. *Al-Tamhîd fî Uṣûl al-Fiqh*. Edited by

Mufîd Abû 'Amsha and Muḥammad b. 'Alî b. Ibrâhîm. 4 vols. Jeddah: Dâr al-Madanî, 1985

al-Kankûhî, Muḥammad Fayḍ. *'Umdat al-Ḥawâshî* (Printed in the margins of *Uṣûl al-Shâshî*). Beirut: Dâr al-Kitâb al-'Arabîya, 1982.

al-Karkhî, Abû Ḥasan 'Ubayd Allâh. *Uṣûl al-Karkhî*. Printed with Dabbûsî's *Ta'sîs al-Naẓar*.

al-Kasânî, Abû Bakr b. Mas'ûd. *Kitâb Badâ'i' al-Ṣanâ'i' fî Tartîb al-Sharâ'i'*. 7 vols. Beirut: Dâr al-Kitâb al-'Arabî, 1982.

Khalîfa, Ḥâjî. *Kashf al-Ẓunûn 'an Asâmî al-Kutub wa al-Funûn*. 6 vols. Damascus: Dâr al-Fikr, 1982.

al-Khallâf, 'Abd al-Wahhâb. *Maṣâdir al-Tashrî' al-Islâmî fî mâ lâ Naṣṣ fîhi*. Kuwait: Dâr al-Qalam, 1978.

_____. *Uṣûl al-Fiqh*. Kuwait: Dâr al-Qalam, 1978.

al-Khunn, Muṣṭafâ. *Athar al-Ikhtilâf fî al-Qawâ'id al-Uṣûlîyyah fî Ikhtilâf al-Fuqahâ'*. Beirut: Mu'assisat al-Risâlah, 1972.

al-Khuḍarî, Muḥammad b. 'Afîfî al-Bâjûrî. *Uṣûl al-Fiqh*. Sixth edition. Cairo: Al-Maktaba al-Tijârîyya, 1969.

_____. *Târîkh al-Tashrî' al-Islâmî*. Eighth edition. n.p.: Dâr al-Fikr, 1967.

Lane, Edward. *An Arabic-English Lexicon*. 8 vols. (parts). Beirut: Librairie du Liban, 1980.

Madkûr, Muḥammad Sallâm. *Al-Ḥukm al-Takhyîrî or Naẓarîyyat al-Ibâḥa 'ind al-Uṣûlîyyîn wa al-Fuqahâ'*. 3d ed. Cairo: Dâr al-Nahḍa al-'Arabîyya, 1965.

_____. *Al-Janîn wa al-Aḥkâm al-Muta'alliqatu bihi fî al-Fiqh al-Islâmî*. Cairo: Dâr al-Nahḍa al-'Arabîyya, 1969.

_____. *Manâhij al-Ijtihâd fî al-Islâm*. Kuwait: Kuwait University Press, 1974.

al-Mahdî, al-Wâfî. *Al-Ijtihâd fî al-Sharî'a al-Islâmîyya*. Al-Dâr al-Bayḍâ' al-Maghrib: Dâr al-Thaqâf, 1984.

Mâlik b. Anas. *Al-Muwaṭṭa'* 2 vols. Edited by Muḥammad 'Abd al-Bâqî n.p.: Dâr al-Turâth al-'Arabî, n.d.

al-Marghinânî, Burhân al-Dîn Abû al-Ḥasan 'Alî b. Abû Bakr. *Al-Hidâyah*. 4 vols. Cairo: Maṭba'at Muṣṭafâ al-Ḥalabî, n.d.

Mas'ûd, Muḥammad Khâlid. *Islamic Legal Philosophy: A Study of Abû Isḥâq al-Shâṭibî's Life and Thought*. Islambad: Islamic Research Institute, 1977.

Ministry of Awqâf & Islamic Affiars of Kuwait. *Mu'jam al-Fiqh al-Ḥanbalî*. 2 vols. Kuwait: Ministry of Awqâf and Islamic Affairs, 1973.

Ministry of Awqâf and Islamic Affiars of Kuwait. *Al-Mawsû'a al-Fiqhîyya*. 3 vols. Kuwait: Ministry of Awqâf and Islamic Affairs, 1982

Muslim b. al-Ḥajjâj, al-Qushayrî. *Ṣaḥîḥ*. 5 vols. Cairo, 1955-56.

_____. *Ṣaḥîḥ Muslim*. 18 vols. 2nd edition. Beirut: Dar Iḥyâ' al-Turâth al-'Arabî, 1972.

Muṣṭafâ, Ibrâhîm; Ḥâmid 'Abd al-Qâdir, Aḥmad Ḥasan al-Zayât; and al-Najâr, Muḥammad 'Alî. *Al-Mu'jam al-Wasîṭ*. 2 vols. Tehran: Maktabat al-'Ilmîyya, n.d.

al-Nawawî, Mûḥî al-Dîn Abû Zakarîyyâ. *Takmilat al-Majmû' Sharḥ al-Muhadhdhab*. 20 vols. Madîna: Al-Maktaba al-Salafîyya, n.d.

al-Pazdawî, Fakhr al-Islâm 'Alî Muḥammad. *Uṣûl Fakhr al-Islâm al-Pazdawî*. Printed on the margin of Bukhârî's *Kashf al-Asrâr*.

Qal'ajî, Muḥammad and Qunaybî, Ḥâmid. *Mu'jam Lughat al-Fuqahâ'*. Beirut: Dâr al-Nafâ'is, 1985.

al-Qarâfî, Aḥmad b. Idrîs. *Al-Iḥkâm fî Tamyîz al-Fatâwâ 'an al-Aḥkâm wa Taṣarrufât al-Qâḍî wa al-Imâm*. Edited by 'Abd al-Fattâḥ Abû Ghudda. Allepo: Maktab al-Maṭbu'ât al-Islâmîyya, 1967.

_____. *Sharḥ Tanqîḥ al-Fuṣûl fî Ikhtiṣâr al-Maḥṣûl*. Cairo: Maṭba'at al-Khayrîyya, 1306 H.

al-Rabî'â, 'Abd al-'Azîz. *Al-Sabab 'ind al-Uṣûlîyyîn*. 3 vols. Riyâḍ: Muḥammad b. Sa'ûd University Press, 1980.

al-Râzî, Fakhr al-Dîn. *Al-Maḥṣûl fî 'ilm Uṣûl al-Fiqh*. 2. vols. Edited by Ṭahâ Jâbir al-Ulwânî. Riyâḍ: Islamic University of Imâm Muḥammad b. Sa'ûd, 1980.

Ṣadr al-Sharî‘a al-Maḥbûbî. *Al-Tawḍîḥ li al-Tanqîḥ*. Printed on the margin of Taftâzânî's *Sharḥ al-Talwîḥ*. 2 vols. Cairo: Dâr al-‘Ahd al-Jadîd li al-Ṭibâ‘a, n.d.

Saḥnûn, b. Sa‘îd al-Tanûkhî. *Al-Mudawwana al-Kubrâ*. 6 vols. Cairo: Maṭba‘at al-Sa‘âda, 1323 H.

al-Sa‘îd, ‘Abd al-‘Azîz. *Ibn Qudâmâ wa Âthârû al-Uṣûlîyya*. 2 vols. Riyâḍ: Muḥammad b. Sa‘ûd University Press, 1979.

Ṣâliḥ, Muḥammad Adîb. *Tafsîr al-al-Nuṣûṣ fî al-Fiqh al-Islâmî*. 2 vols. Beirut: Al-Maktab al-Islâmî, n.d.

Ṣâliḥ, Ṣubḥî. *Uṣûl al-Ḥadîth*. 9th ed. Beirut: Dâr al-‘Ilm li Malâyîn, 1977.

al-Sarakhsî, Shams al-A'immah Abû Bakr Muḥammad. *Al-Mabsûṭ*. 30 vols. Beirut: Dâr al-Ma‘rifa, 1978.

____. *Uṣûl al-Sarakhsî*. 2 vols. Edited by Abû al-Wafâ' al-Afghânî. Beirut: Dâr al-Ma‘rifa, n.d.

al-Shâfi‘î, Muḥammad b. Idrîs. *Al-Risâla*. Edited by Aḥmad M. Shâkir. Cairo: Dâr al-Turâth, 1979.

_____. *Al-Umm*. 7 vols. Cairo: Kitâb al-Sha‘b, n.d.

Shalabî, Muḥammad Muṣṭafâ. *Al-Madkhal fî al-Ta‘rîf bi al-Fiqh al-Islâmî*. Beirut: Dâr al-Nahḍa al-‘Arabîyya, 1969.

_____. *Uṣûl al-Fiqh al-*. Beirut: Dâr al-Nahḍa al-‘Arabîyya, 1978.

al-Shâṭibî, Abû Isḥâq. *al-I‘tiṣâm*. 2 vols. Beirut: Dâr al-Ma‘rifa, n.d.

_____. *al-Muwâfaqât*. 4 vols. Edited by ‘Abd Allâh Drâz. Beirut: Dâr al-Ma‘rifa, n.d.

al-Shawkânî, Muhammad b. ‘Alî. *Irshâd al-Fuḥûl ilâ Taḥqîq al-Ḥaqq min ‘Ilm al-Uṣûl*. Cairo: Muṣṭafâ al-Halabî Press, 1356 H.

_____. *Nayl al-Awṭâr*. 9 vols. Beirut: Dâr al-Jîl, 1973.

al-Shirâzî, Abû Isḥâq Ibrâhîm.b. ‘Alî b. Yûsuf al-Fayrûzabâdî. *Ṭabaqât al-Fuqahâ'*. Edited by Iḥsân ‘Abbâs. Beirut: Dâr al-Râ'id al-‘Arabî, 1981.

____. Edited by Muḥammad Ḥasan Hîtû. Damascus: Dâr al-Fikr, 1980.

al-Siyûṭî, Jalâl al-Dîn 'Abd al-Raḥmân. *al-Dûr al-Manthûr fî al-Tafsîr bi al-Ma'thûr*. Beirut: Dâr al-Fikr, 1983.

al-Subkî, 'Abd al-Wahhâb b. 'Alî and al-Subkî, 'Alî. *al-Ibhâj fî Sharḥ al-Minhâj*. 3 vols. Beirut: Dâr al-Kutub al-'Ilmîyya, 1984.

_____. *Ṭabaqât al-Shâfi'îyya al-Kubrâ*. 10 vols. Edited by 'Abd al-Fattâḥ al-Ḥulû and Maḥmûd al-Tanâhî. Cairo: Al-Ḥalabî Press, 1966.

al-Ṭabarî, Abû Ja'far Muḥammad b. Jarîr. *Jâmi' al-Bayân 'an Ta'wîl 'ây al-Qur'ân*. 30 vols. (in 12) 3d edition. Cairo: Al-Ḥalabî Press, 1968.

_____. *Ikhtilâf al-Fuqahâ'*. 2nd edition. Beirut, 1902.

al-Taftâzânî, Sa'd al-Dîn. *Sharḥ al-Talwîḥ 'alâ al-Tawḍîḥ*. 2 vols. Cairo: Dâr al-'Ahd al-Jadîd li al-Ṭibâ'a, n.d.

al-Tahânawî, M. *Kashshâf Istilâhât al-Funûn*. Edited A. Sprenger. 2 vols. Calcutta, 1854; reprinted. Istanbul: Dâr Qahrmân, 1984.

al-Tirmidhî, Muḥammad b. 'Isâ. *Sunan al-Tirmidhî*. 10 vols. Cairo: Al-Ḥalabî Press, 1965-68.

al-'Umarî, Nâdîyya. *al-Ijtihâd fî al-Islâm*. Beirut: Mu'assasa al-Risâla, 1981.

_____. *al-Naskh fî Dirâsât al-Uṣûlîyyîn*. Beirut: Mu'assasa al-Risâla, 1980.

Wensinck, A. J. *Concordance et Indices de la Traditione Musulmane*. 7 vols. Leiden: E.J. Brill, 1936-1969.

al-Zabîdî, Muḥammad Murtaḍa al-Ḥusaynî. *Itḥâf al-Sâda al-Muttaqîn bi Sharḥ Asrâr Iḥyâ' 'Ulûm al-Dîn*. 10 vols. Cairo, '1311/1894.

_____. *Tâj al-'Arûs*. 10 vols. Cairo: Khayrîyya Press, 1306.

al-Zaḥîlî, Wahba. *Al-Fiqh al-Islâmî wa Adillatuh*. 2nd ed. 8 vols. Damascus: Dâr al-Fikr,1985.

al-Zamakhsharî, M. b. 'Umar. *Al-Kashshâf 'an Ḥaqâ'iq Ghawâmiḍ al-Tanzîl wa 'Uyûn al-Aqâwîl fî Wujûh al-Ta'wîl*. 4 vols. Beirut: Dâr al-Ma'rifa, 1947; rpt., n.d.

al-Zarqâ, Muṣṭafâ. *Al-Madkhal al-Fiqhî al-'Âmm*. 3 vols. Damascus: Maṭba'at Alif Ba', 1967-68.

al-Zâwî, al-Ṭâhir Aḥmad. *Tartîb al-Qâmûs*. 2nd ed. 4 vols. Beirut: Dâr al-Fikr, n.d..

Zaydân, 'Abd al-Karîm. *Aḥkâm al-Dhimmîyyîn wa al-Must'amînîn fî Dâr al-Islâm*. Baghdâd: University of Baghdâd, 1963.

Zayla'î, Jamâl al-Dîn Abî Muḥammad 'Abd Allâh b. Yûsuf al-Ḥanafî. *Nasb al-Râyyah li Aḥâdîth al-Hidâya*. 4 vols. 2d ed. n.p.: Al-Maktaba al-Islâmîyya, 1973.

al-Ziriklî, Khayr al-Dîn. *Al-A'lâm Qâmûs Tarâjum*. 8 vols. Beirut: Dâr al-'Ilm li al-Malâyîn, 1980.

ACKNOWLEDGMENTS

I would like to acknowledge the efforts of Amer Haleem and Ibrahim Abusharif for their professional help in preparing the text for publication, as well as Ibrahim Abdul Aziz for helping with part of the first draft of the translation. Earnest appreciation goes to my dear friend, Brother Gaylord Toft, whose insistence to make optimal use of current computer technology has saved a tremendous amount of time for this and other projects. May Allah bless him and his family. Also, appreciation is extended to Dr. Abdul Hakim S. Jackson and Saleem Kayani for reading the text and offering insightful suggestions.

Ahmad Zaki Hammad

INDEX